For Tricia, Van Morrison and my father
"...as big as a whale's love can be."

This edition is published by special arrangement with Dell, a division of
Bantam Doubleday Dell Publishing Group, Inc.

Grateful acknowledgment is made to Dell, a division of Bantam Doubleday
Dell Publishing Group, Inc. for permission to reprint *My Friend Whale* by
Simon James. Copyright © 1990 by Simon James.

Printed in the United States of America

ISBN 0-15-302117-9

4 5 6 7 8 9 10   035   97 96 95

MY FRIEND WHALE

Simon James

HARCOURT BRACE & COMPANY

Orlando Atlanta Austin Boston San Francisco Chicago Dallas New York
Toronto London

My friend Whale and I swim together every night.

My friend Whale is a blue whale.

My friend Whale makes the biggest splash of any sea creature,

but he is a very slow and graceful swimmer.

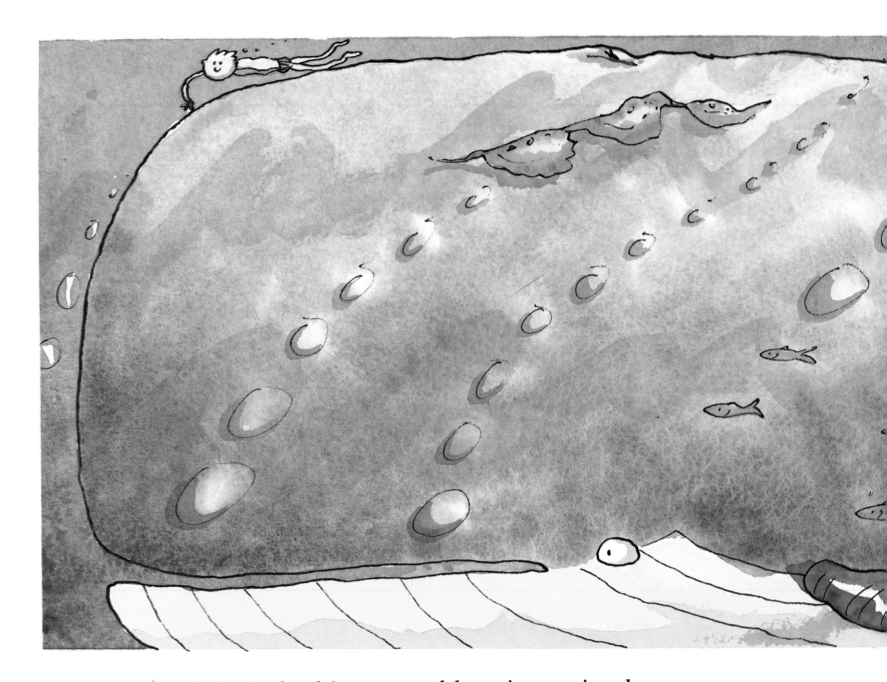

My friend Whale is the biggest and heaviest animal on land or in the sea.

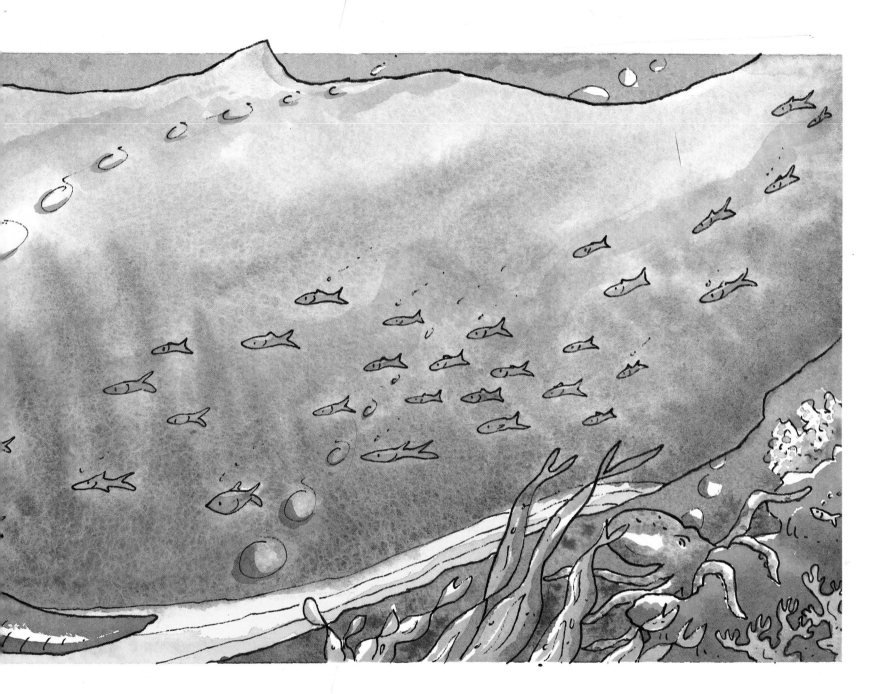

You may think, because he is so large, that he must be dangerous.

But my friend Whale has no teeth.

In fact, he only eats fishy things smaller than my little finger.

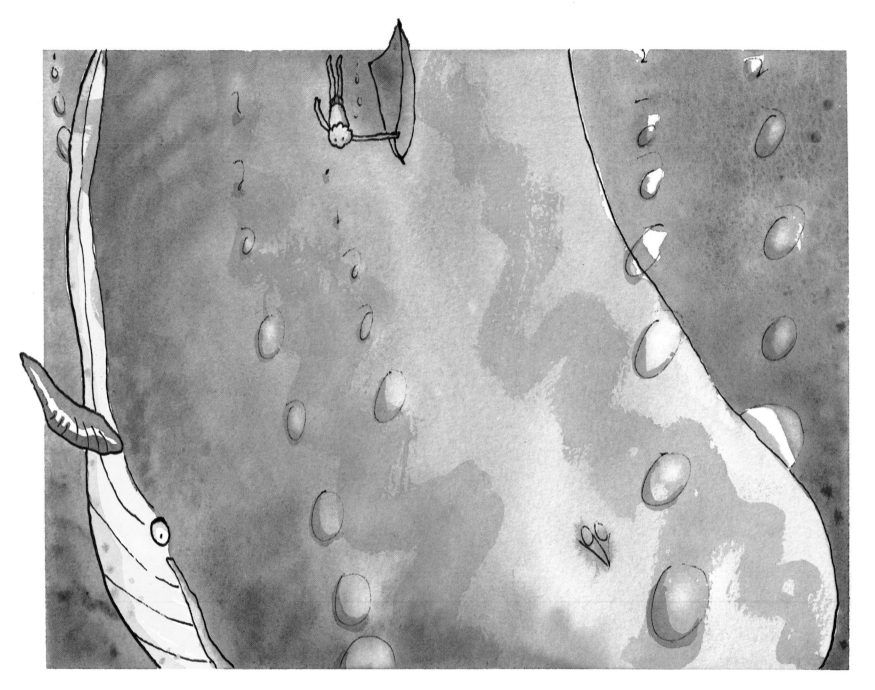

My friend Whale can hold his breath underwater for almost an hour.

But because he is not a fish, he has to come up for air just like me.

My friend Whale can't smell anything.
My friend Whale can't taste anything.

But he has very good ears –
he can hear an underwater world of things that I can't.

My friend Whale speaks with squeaking, clicking, and whistling sounds.

Other whales can hear him from a hundred miles away.

My friend Whale has very sensitive skin.
He can feel the slightest touch.

That is the way I say good-bye for the night.
See you tomorrow, my friend Whale.

My friend Whale really does make the biggest splash. But the next night, I don't see the spray of his spout or the splash of his tail.

He didn't come for me at all.

My friend Whale didn't come last night either, or the night before. Maybe he's found a new friend.

Or maybe something has happened to him.
Now my friend Whale only visits in my dreams.